THE JAGS

Who's Got My Boots?

TOM WATT

Rising Stars UK Ltd.
7 Hatchers Mews, Bermondsey Street, London SE1 3GS
www.risingstars-uk.com

Published 2009
Reprinted 2010, 2012, 2013, 2014

Publisher: Gill Budgell
Editor: Jane Wood
Text design and typesetting: Clive Sutherland
Illustrator: Michael Emmerson for Advocate Art
Cover design: Burville-Riley Partnership
Cover photograph: Ron Coello at www.coellophotography.co.uk
With special thanks to; Robert Dye, Harry Garner, Tyrone Smith, Lewis
McKenzie, Kobina Crankson and Alex Whyte

British Library Cataloguing in Publication Data.
A CIP record for this book is available from the British Library.

ISBN: 978-1-84680-476-2
Printed in the UK by Ashford Colour Press Ltd

Contents

Map

Jeffers

Chu...

Middleton School

The Burton Twins

Nev

Kilderton

Fozzer

The Rec

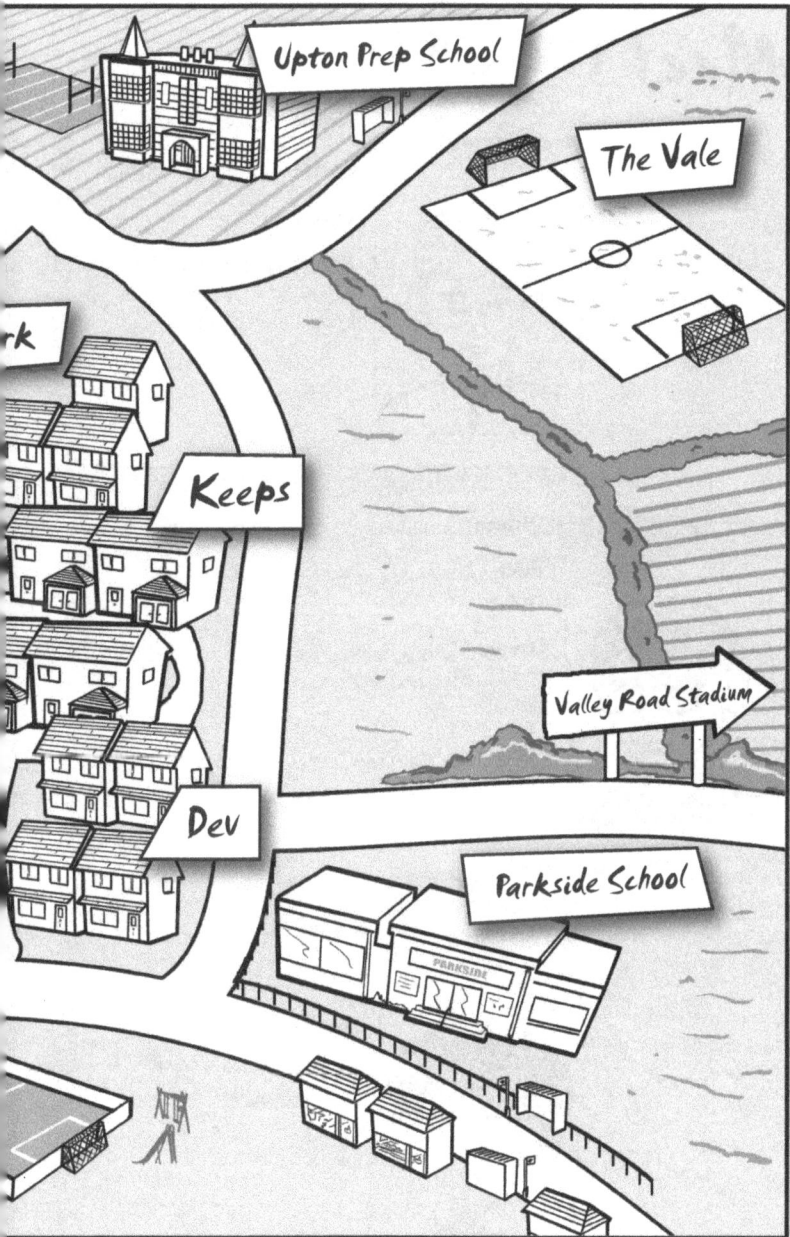

Upton Prep School

The Vale

rk

Keeps

Dev

Valley Road Stadium

Parkside School

PARKSIDE

Meet the Jags

Name: Andrew Burton

Fact: He's the Jags' captain.

Loves: Spurs

FYI: The Jags may be his mates, but they'd better not forget he's the Skipper.

Andy

Name: Terry Burton

Fact: He's Andy's twin brother.

Loves: Football, football, and more football. He's football crazy!

FYI: He's a big Arsenal fan.

Burts

Name: Ryan Devlin

Fact: He's very forgetful.

Loves: Daydreaming!

FYI: He's always covered in mud and bruises.

Dev

Name: Hamed Foster

Fact: He can run like crazy, but he shoots like crazy too – sometimes at the wrong goal!

Loves: Telling bad jokes.

FYI: His best friend is Nev.

Fozzer

Name: Jim Ward

Fact: He's the Jags' Number One goalie – whether he likes it or not!

Loves: Trying to score from his end of the pitch.

FYI: He's the tallest member of the Jags.

Keeps

Name: Jeffrey Gilfoyle Chapman

Fact: He's the only one of the Jags who doesn't live on the Chudley Park estate.

Loves: Being in the Jags.

FYI: He's the Jags' top goal-scorer.

Jeffers

Nev

Name: Denton Neville

Fact: Nev is the Jags' most talented player.

Loves: Fozzer's bad jokes.

FYI: He keeps his feet on the ground and always looks out for his football crazy mates.

Mrs Burton

Name: Pam Burton

Fact: The Burton twins' mum, and a team 'mum' for all the Jags.

Loves: Sorting out her boys.

FYI: Doesn't actually like football!

Mr Ward

Name: Jack Ward

Fact: He's Jim's dad and the Jags' coach!

Loves: Going on and on, doing his team talks.

FYI: He's taking his coaching exams.

Wakey-Wakey!

It all started one Friday night when Dev and I were walking home from school together.

Keeps   I can't wait for Sunday morning.

Dev   I know. I like a long lie-in. Mum will have recorded *Match of the Day* for me.

Keeps Eh? Aren't you forgetting something?

Dev Oh, yeah. I'll have my toast on the sofa while I'm watching.

Keeps Watching? We're playing! That mini-tournament at The Vale!

Dev How could I forget? The Jags against the rest of Kilderton!

Keeps   Wakey-wakey!

Dev   Great! What time do we have to be there again?

Keeps   Nine o'clock. My dad will bring the kit. Just bring your boots.

My boots? Where are my boots?

Keeps	Dev! What are you doing?
Dev	My boots. I don't know where my boots are.
Keeps	Did you leave them at school?
Dev	I don't know. Let's go and see before Mrs Jones goes home!

Keeps   Come on, let's run. We need the training!

Dev   What if I can't find them?

Keeps   Get some new ones?

Dev   I've been saving up but I still need another £2.

Keeps   Look! There's Mrs Jones. We're just in time.

Dev   Oh, Mrs Jones! I'm really pleased to see you. Can we come back into school?

2

Oh, No! Underpants!

Mrs Jones gave Dev a funny look when he said he was pleased to see her. But she let us in anyway.

Keeps Mrs Jones says we can look in the Lost and Found box if we don't make a mess.

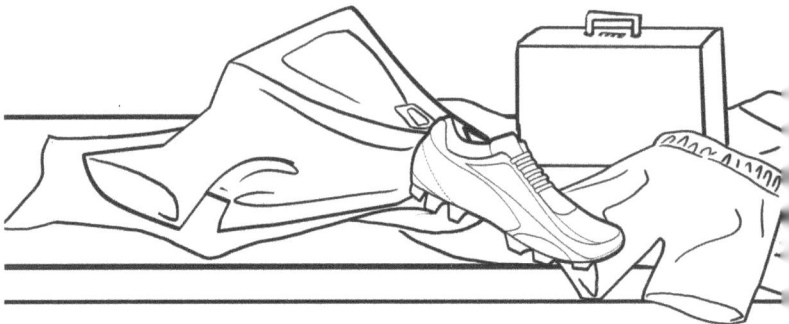

Dev But the Lost and Found box is already a mess. And it smells. Do you think we need rubber gloves on? Urggh! This sock is all wet. And it's got green bits.

Keeps   I think that's what Mrs Jones
meant when she said no mess.
She likes to keep all the mess in
one place. Can you see your
boots?

Dev   Well, here's one boot. But I
don't think it's mine, do you?

Keeps   That's a very big boot.

Dev   Big? It's huge! Look, it says size
12. I didn't know Kanu went to
our school!

Keeps I wish he did go to Parkside. What a player. If he was playing for the Jags, we'd win every game!

Dev Oh, no! Underpants! Is this the Lost and Found box or the washing basket? I feel sick.

Keeps Me too. But what about your boots?

Dev I've found one size 12 and an old pair of underpants, so far.

Keeps   Look out! Mrs Jones wants to see how we are getting on!

Dev   It's okay, Mrs Jones! We are just looking for my boots!

Keeps   Shhh! Don't let her come in. Look at the mess.

Keeps   We'd better tidy up. Your boots aren't here, are they?

Dev   No. Maybe they're at home.

Keeps   Why didn't you say so? I need a bath now, or I'll stink for the rest of the day!

Special Offer!
Today Only!

We passed the football kit shop on our way back to Dev's house. And we had to look in.

Keeps   Look, Dev! Kit Direct has got a sale on!

Dev   I know. But I still haven't got enough for new boots.

Keeps   How do you know? The ones you want might be in the sale.

Keeps   Hey, Dev. Look at these.
They're half price.

Dev   Yeah, but they're still £50. It's
always the same. They have a
sale but the thing you want is
still too much.

Keeps   They're all white, like the ones Fernando Torres wears.

Dev   You'd have to be Fernando Torres to afford them!

Keeps   What about these? I wonder if they have got my size.

Dev   What? Blue boots? You have to be a very good player to play in blue boots.

Keeps   Are you saying I'm not a very good player?

Dev   No. I'm just saying you're a goalkeeper. Remember? Did you ever see a goalkeeper in blue boots?

Keeps   Mmm. Maybe not.

Dev   Anyway, this isn't finding my boots.

Keeps   No. But if they're at your house, there's no rush.

Dev   These are the ones I want. Just good old black lace-up boots with studs for grip. They're cheap, too. But good.

CHEAP BUT GOOD

Keeps Well, what are you waiting for?

Dev I told you. I still need another £2.

Does he ever listen to a word I say?

Keeps We'd better find your old boots then, hadn't we?

Dev Yeah. Are you going to help?

④

Follow the Footprints

So, we got to Dev's house and there was a note on the door. It said:

> Gone to visit Auntie Jill.
> See you later.

Dev Oh, no. I thought Mum would know where to find my boots.

Keeps How long will she be?

Dev Who knows? Once she and my auntie get talking, there's no stopping them.

Dev Oh, no! I remember now!

Keeps Remember what? Where your boots are?

Dev I remember why Mum's going to go mad at me!

Keeps Look at this mess. It looks like someone has run around your house in football boots!

Dev   Someone *has* run around my
house in football boots.

Keeps   Who?

Dev   Me, of course. I was playing
football in the garden before
school. I didn't notice the time.
Then I was late so I had to run
in to get changed.

Keeps The mess goes all the way up here. Look! That's great.

Dev What do you mean, "That's great"?

Keeps We just have to follow the mess to find your boots … and here they are. Now you can play in the tournament on Sunday.

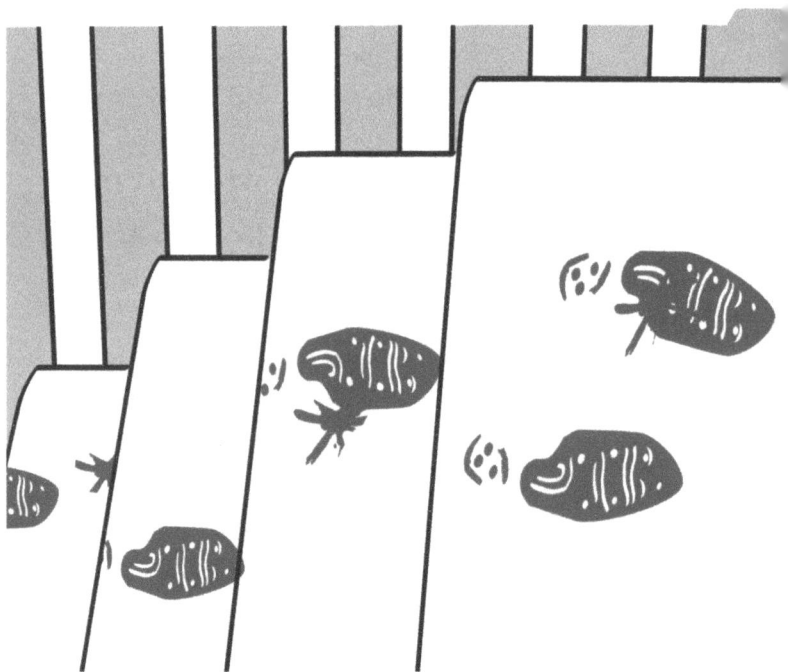

Dev   You don't get it. I'm in big trouble. Mum will go mad about this mess. She might not *let* me play on Sunday.

Keeps   What are you going to do?

Dev   I'm going to get some water.

Keeps   What for? To clean your boots?

Dev   No. To clean the floor. If I don't, there's no point cleaning my boots.

Dev's right. There's no point cleaning these boots. It's only the mud that's holding them together!

Dev   Don't just sit there, Keeps. Get me some more hot water.

Keeps   I'm just thinking about how to get your new boots. These old boots have had it, you know.

New Boots for Old

> *I went home, hoping Dev's mum would let him play on Sunday. The Jags would be in trouble in a seven-a-side tournament if there were only six of us.*
> *When we met up the next day, I could see Dev had some good news.*

Dev   Hello, Keeps. What a lovely day, eh?

Keeps   Are you all right, Dev? What did your mum say?

Dev   What did she say about what?

Keeps   What did she say about the
                 mess? Will she let you play?

Dev   Those boots won't ever make a mess again. Mum threw them away.

Keeps   Oh, no. What are you going to do on Sunday?

Dev   Wear my new ones, of course. Look!

Keeps   Those are the ones you wanted. The cheap but good ones. But how did you get them?

Dev I didn't get them. My mum got them.

Keeps What did your mum get a pair of football boots for? She doesn't play football.

Dev They're not for her, are they? She got them for me. She was so happy with me for cleaning up the mess that she gave me the £2 that I needed to buy the new ones.

Keeps   But wasn't she angry with you for making a mess in the first place?

Dev   She would have been but …

Keeps   Us cleaning up saved the day. Maybe you should give me half the money for helping you.

What do you mean? You didn't help me at all!

Keeps   Well, I helped you look for your old boots, didn't I?

Dev   Yeah. But I cleaned up all on my own. You were "thinking" about how to get me my new boots!

Keeps That's true. But sometimes the best way to help is to do the thinking. As in …

JAGUARS 1 RIVER REDS 1
(Jags win on penalties)

Thank goodness Dev got his new boots. He was the Jags' star player at the tournament. We played the Kilder Ravens and the Town Boys' Club. We drew the first game. Then Dev got the winner in the last minute against the Boys' Club to put us in the final against the River Reds.

Dev   What a goal!

Keeps   Great ball, Dev. Come on the
        Jags!

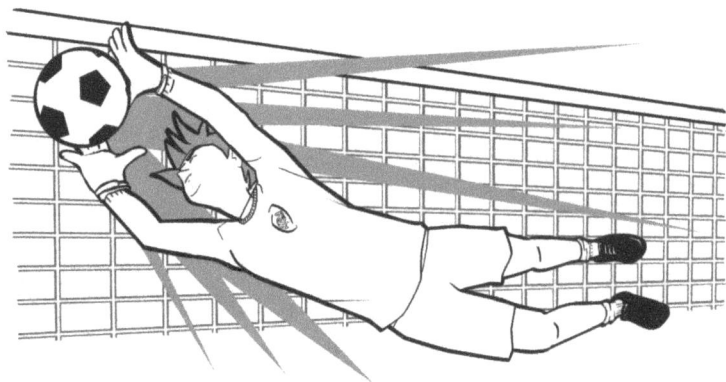

Dev   Jaguars, Jaguars Number One!
        Jaguars Number One! What a
        save, Keeps!

Keeps   Thanks. It was great how you all
        stuck your spot kicks away, too.

My new boots felt great. We got to the final. It was 1–1 and then we won it on penalties. Me, Nev, Fozzer and Burts all scored ours and Keeps kept out the penalty by the River Reds' star striker. What a keeper! What a day!

The Boot Story

A hundred years ago, football boots looked just like work boots. They were big and heavy and often had steel toecaps. They had studs nailed into the sole to give a better grip.

Later on, the boots were not so heavy. They were cut lower, too, so the player's foot could move more easily.

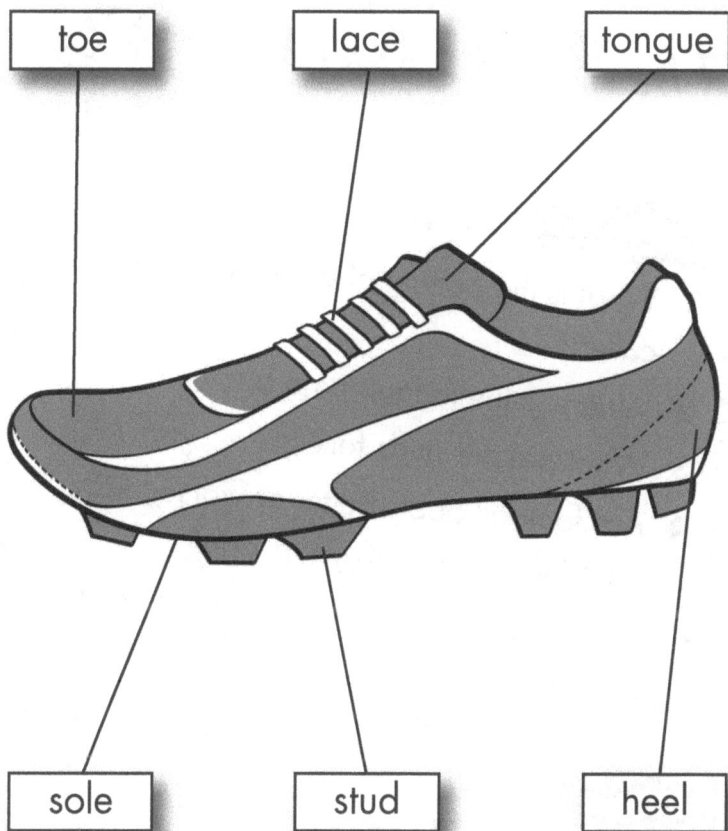

toe | lace | tongue

sole | stud | heel

Now, football boots are very light. They have screw-in studs or blades. You can get special boots for playing on hard ground or AstroTurf.

Players now get more foot injuries because the boots aren't so tough.

The Boots Quiz

Questions

1 What is the bottom of a football boot called?

2 Where is the tongue on a boot?

3 What are the studs for?

4 Are football boots better or worse today than they were 100 years ago?

Answers

1 The sole.

2 On the top.

3 To give better grip.

4 Both! Better, because they aren't so heavy and you can move your feet more easily. Worse, because they aren't so tough and you get more foot injuries.

About the Author

Tom Watt, who writes the Jags books, loves playing football. He used to run a charity team called the Walford Boys' Club with ex-pros and TV stars. He's really old now, but he still likes to play against his son in the back garden. His son usually wins.

Tom's best-ever football boots were made by a firm called Patrick. They were from France, but they didn't help Tom play like Thierry Henry. In fact, it didn't really matter which boots he wore. He still scored own goals!

THE JAGS

Who's Got My Boots?
A New Striker
The Derby Match
Who's Washing the Kit?
The Big Deal
Star Player Wanted
Your Turn in Goal
The Team Talk
Whose Side Are You On?
Hitting the Headlines
Up for the Cup
The Own Goal

RISING STARS

The Jags books are available from most book sellers.
For mail order information
please call Rising Stars on 0800 091 1602
or visit www.risingstars-uk.com